Countries Around the World

Canada

Michael Hurley

Heinemann Library
Chicago, Illinois

www.capstonepub.com
Visit our website to find out more information about Heinemann-Raintree books.

To order:
☎ Phone 888-454-2279
🖳 Visit www.capstonepub.com to browse our catalog and order online.

Edited by Catherine Veitch and Charlotte Guillain
Designed by Steve Mead
Original illustrations © Capstone Global Library Ltd 2012
Illustrated by Oxford Designers & Illustrators
Picture research by Hannah Taylor
Originated by Capstone Global Library Ltd
Printed and bound in China by CTPS

15 14
10 9 8 7 6 5 4 3 2

Library of Congress Cataloging-in-Publication Data
Hurley, Michael.
  Canada / Michael Hurley.
    p. cm.—(Countries around the world)
  Includes bibliographical references and index.
  ISBN 978-1-4329-6095-7 (hb)—ISBN 978-1-4329-6121-3 (pb) 1.
Canada—Juvenile literature. I. Title.
  F1008.2.H87 2012
  97.—dc22   2011015801

Acknowledgments
We would like to thank the following for permission to reproduce photographs: The Art Archive p. 9 (National Army Museum London); Bridgeman Art Library pp. 6 (Art Gallery of Ontario, Toronto, Canada), 10 (Private Collection/Peter Newark American Pictures), 29 (Art Gallery of Ontario, Toronto, Canada/The Bridgeman Art Library); Corbis pp. 7 (National Geographic Society), 23 (Juice Images), 26 (Marie-Reine Mattera), 31 (Bettmann); Getty Images pp. 8 (Stock Montage), 11 (Hulton Archive), 19 (All Canada Photos/ Dave Reede), 28 (Bryan Bedder); istockphoto p. 20 (© Roberto A Sanchez); Photolibrary pp. 13 (All Canada Photos/Oleksiy Maksymenko), 27 (Kristy-Anne Glubish); Shutterstock pp. 5 (© Niv Koren), 15 (© Pi-Lens), 17 (© kwest), 21 (© Keith Levit), 24 (© Zoran Karapancev), 25 (© Elena Elisseeva), 30 (© Debby Wong), 32 (© GoodMood Photo), 35 (© Karen Gentry), 39 (© Helga Esteb).

Cover photograph of a train, Morant's Curve, Banff National Park, Alberta, Canada, reproduced with permission of Photolibrary (Tom Nevesely).

Every effort has been made to contact copyright holders of material reproduced in this book. Any omissions will be rectified in subsequent printings if notice is given to the publisher.

The publishers would like to thank Professor Emily Gilbert for her assistance in the preparation of this book.

Disclaimer
All the Internet addresses (URLs) given in this book were valid at the time of going to press. However, due to the dynamic nature of the Internet, some addresses may have changed, or sites may have changed or ceased to exist since publication. While the author and publisher regret any inconvenience this may cause readers, no responsibility for any such changes can be accepted by either the author or the publisher.

Contents

Some words in the book are in bold, **like this**. You can find out what they mean by looking in the glossary.

Introducing Canada

What comes to mind when you think of Canada? Do you see the Canadian flag, with its red maple leaf? Do you think about big cities, or large areas of wilderness? Do you picture an image of the famous Canadian Mounties on horseback? Perhaps you think about the Great Lakes that stretch across the border with the United States?

Second largest

Canada is a relatively young country. It became a nation in 1867, after many years of war between British and French **settlers**. Canada is the second-largest country in the world, and it is part of the continent of North America. It has an area of more than 3,855,103 square miles (9,984,670 square kilometers). Only Russia is larger.

More than 33 million people live in Canada. People live mostly in the southern part of the country, near the border with the United States. Around 90 percent of the population lives within 100 miles (160 kilometers) of this border. The northern part of Canada is very cold all year round, and very few people live there. The **indigenous** people who do live there are known as Inuit.

Stunning scenery

Canada is an enormous and varied country full of stunning scenery, including dramatic coastlines, mountain ranges, glaciers, rivers, and lakes. Canada has approximately two million lakes! It is a country rich in **natural resources** such as oil, coal, gold, diamonds, and copper.

Surrounded by the beautiful natural landscape, people can have fun canoeing on one of Canada's many lakes.

History: Conflict and Change

Humans have lived in North America for around 20,000 years. Over time, these people settled all over Canada and what is now the United States. There were many different **tribes**, including the Huron and Dene.

These early tribes spent their time making tools and hunting for food. Coastal people caught fish, while the people living further inland hunted animals such as **caribou** and musk ox for meat. These **indigenous** people lived in this way for more than 12,000 years before any other **settlers** arrived in Canada. These tribes are now known as native Canadians, or First Nations.

This painting from the 1800s shows members of the Huron tribe camped by Lake Huron.

How to say...

The word "Canada" comes from the Huron and Iroquois word "*kanata.*" "*Kanata*" means "village" or "settlement."

Vikings arrive

In 1000 CE Vikings from Scandinavia crossed the Atlantic Ocean and landed on the northeast coast of Canada. They set up a **colony** and gave it the name Vinland. The Vikings found the landscape on the northeast coast harsh and difficult to settle. They soon returned to Scandinavia.

Voyages of discovery

In 1497 an Italian named John Cabot, working on behalf of the English King Henry VII, set out across the Atlantic Ocean. He was an experienced sailor and **navigator**. He had planned to find a route to Asia, because at this time there was a valuable trade in spices. After a voyage that lasted nearly two months, he landed his ship on the eastern coast of Canada. Cabot named the area Newfoundland and claimed this new land for England.

This artist's impression shows Vikings from Scandinavia arriving on the east coast of Canada to create a settlement.

"New France"

In 1524 France sent explorers to North America. First Giovanni de Verrazano traveled across the Atlantic, and then Jacques Cartier followed in 1534. In 1535 Jacques Cartier made a second voyage, this time with three shiploads of French settlers to set up a colony. However, after a bitterly cold winter killed many settlers, the idea was abandoned.

The first Europeans to settle permanently came from France in the 1600s. They called the territory "New France." Samuel de Champlain founded Quebec City in 1608. The British also returned to Canada and set up their own settlements in different areas.

Conflict

There was rivalry between the French and British settlers, which led to many conflicts. The French and British were also fighting a war against each other in Europe. Battles took place on both sides of the Atlantic Ocean, until the British finally defeated the French. Both countries signed a **treaty** in 1763, giving Britain almost complete control of Canada. In 1774 Britain allowed the area of Quebec to be run by the French.

French sailor and navigator Jacques Cartier (1491–1557) made three journeys to explore the east coast of North America.

How to say...

English and French are the two official languages of Canada.

good morning	*bonjour*	(bon-jure)
hello	*salut*	(sa-loo)
goodbye	*au revoir*	(oh re-vwa)

The British and French also fought with and against native Canadians, who were unhappy about the way their land had been taken. There were violent uprisings, and many people were killed. The rebellion was stopped after Britain sent in more forces. Treaties were signed to bring an end to the conflict.

This artist's impression shows the British and French forces battling with each other for control of Canada in the 1700s.

Becoming a country

Between 1815 and 1850, Canada's population grew to around 800,000. These people—mainly from Britain—settled across the country. Massive areas of forest were destroyed to create farmland for these settlers. The settlers built a basic **infrastructure** of roads and canals to transport people and goods. In 1867 the different colonies united and became one country: Canada. Canada's first **constitution** meant that there was now a central government in Canada with a House of **Parliament**, but each area was responsible for itself. These areas were called provinces. Over the next six years, another three provinces joined the **Confederation**, stretching Canada over to the west coast.

This artwork shows how European settlers traded with indigenous people, mainly for animal furs. The furs were sent to Europe to be turned into fashionable hats and other garments.

Railroads and the gold rush

Because of the huge size of the country, railroads were needed to transport people and goods across the land more efficiently. A network of railroads was built between the growing towns and cities. The transcontinental railroad connected the west coast to the east and was completed in 1885.

In 1896 the Klondike Gold Rush began. A **prospector** who was searching for gold near the Klondike River in the Yukon found a large nugget of the precious **commodity**. The news soon spread, and within two years around 100,000 people had set off in search of their fortunes. Around 40,000 completed the journey, but only a small percentage found any gold.

Prospectors look for gold along the Klondike River. Some of these men traveled long distances in their search for gold.

More fighting

During World War I (1914–1918), Canada sent hundreds of thousands of troops, many of them volunteers, to help the British and French fight against Germany in Europe. More than 60,000 Canadians died during this conflict.

Canada fought alongside the **Allies** during World War II (1939–1945). Many Canadian troops were based in Great Britain. Again, Canada suffered devastating losses, with over 40,000 soldiers killed in action.

Multiculturalism

After World War II, people from many parts of the world came to settle in Canada. Canada introduced an official **multicultural** policy in 1971. This policy aims to recognize and support the increasing **diversity** of the population.

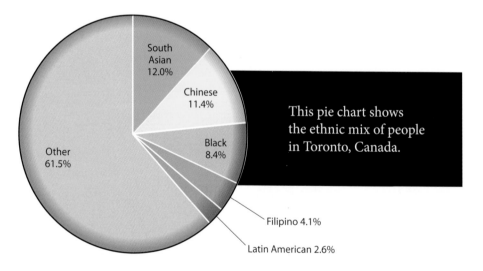

South Asian 12.0%

Chinese 11.4%

Other 61.5%

Black 8.4%

This pie chart shows the ethnic mix of people in Toronto, Canada.

Filipino 4.1%

Latin American 2.6%

KIM CAMPBELL (BORN 1947)

Kim Campbell became a member of parliament in 1988, and in 1990 she was the first woman to be appointed minister of justice and attorney general. In 1993 Campbell became the first female **prime minister** in Canada's history.

Modern Canada

The Canada Act of 1982 ended British control of Canada, giving Canada responsibility for future changes to its constitution. Although it had been mostly **autonomous** since 1867, this new act confirmed Canada as an independent, self-governing country.

For centuries, **immigrants** from other countries have settled in Canada. In recent times immigrants have moved to Canada from all over the world, particularly from Asia and the Middle East. They are attracted by the high standard of living, good quality of life, and opportunities for work.

Toronto is Canada's largest city. It is recognized as one of the most diverse cities in the world.

Regions and Resources: Land of Lakes and Mountains

Canada has a land border with only one other country: the United States. In the northwest of Canada lies the region of Alaska, which is part of the United States. The large island of Greenland lies in the ocean to the east of Canada.

Climate

Canada is mostly wet and warm on the west coast, while in northern regions the temperature hardly rises above freezing. People living in the southern part of Canada can experience very harsh winters. In the summer, this part of Canada enjoys a more **temperate** climate. The east coast of Canada does not get as cold as the rest of the country, but in the winter months the temperature is rarely above freezing.

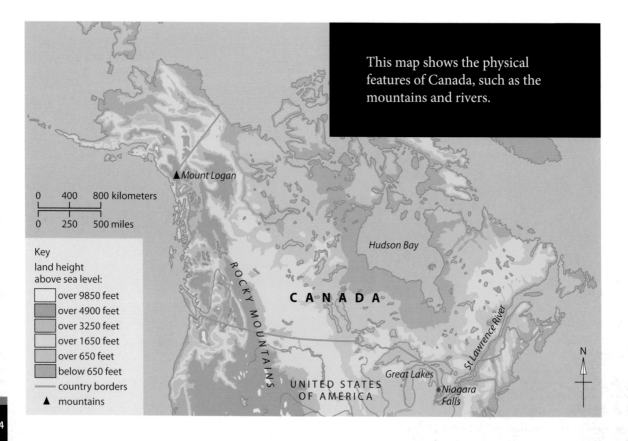

This map shows the physical features of Canada, such as the mountains and rivers.

▲ Mount Logan

| 0 | 400 | 800 kilometers |
| 0 | 250 | 500 miles |

Key
land height
above sea level:

- over 9850 feet
- over 4900 feet
- over 3250 feet
- over 1650 feet
- over 650 feet
- below 650 feet
- — country borders
- ▲ mountains

Hudson Bay

ROCKY MOUNTAINS

CANADA

St Lawrence River

N

Great Lakes

UNITED STATES
OF AMERICA

Niagara
Falls

Key landforms

The Great Lakes are five huge lakes that lie between Canada and the United States, with the national border running through four of these lakes. Lake Superior is the largest lake in the world. Niagara Falls, which is popular with tourists, runs into Lake Ontario. The Mackenzie River is the longest river in Canada.

The Rocky Mountains stretch from the northwest tip of Canada into the United States. The mountain range is 3,000 miles (4,800 kilometers) long. The tallest mountain in Canada is Mount Logan, at 19,551 feet (5,959 meters). It is located in the Yukon Territory, close to the border with Alaska.

Daily life

In the winter, in the far north of Canada, the sun does not rise and the days are dark. In the summer, the sun never totally sets, so the nights are light.

This stunning natural phenomenon, which can be seen in Canada, is called the Aurora Borealis or "Northern Lights." It occurs when electrically charged particles from the sun collide with atoms in Earth's atmosphere.

Territories and provinces

There are 13 different regions that make up Canada: 3 territories and 10 provinces. The three territories, Yukon, Northwest Territories, and Nunavut, are in northern Canada and cover a huge area of land. They are largely self-governed, and the majority of the population in these territories is Inuit.

The 10 provinces of Canada are British Columbia, Alberta, Saskatchewan, Manitoba, Ontario, Quebec, Newfoundland and Labrador, Prince Edward Island, New Brunswick, and Nova Scotia. Quebec is the largest province. Prince Edward Island, off the east coast, is the smallest. Each province and territory has its own capital. The province of Quebec has a large French-speaking population. They have tried unsuccessfully to gain more independence from Canada.

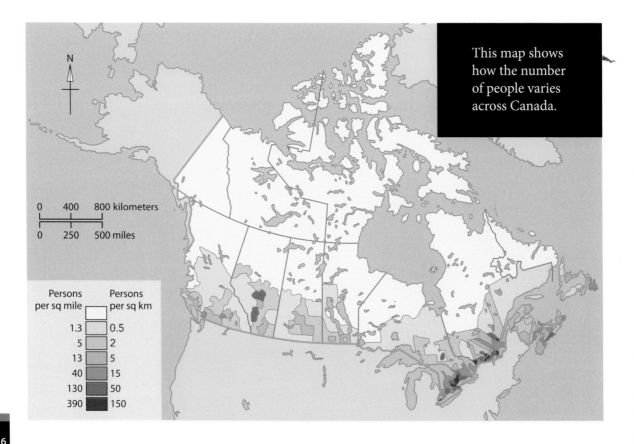

This map shows how the number of people varies across Canada.

N

| 0 | 400 | 800 kilometers |
| 0 | 250 | 500 miles |

Persons per sq mile		Persons per sq km
1.3		0.5
5		2
13		5
40		15
130		50
390		150

Major cities

The capital city of Canada is Ottawa, in the province of Ontario. Ottawa has a population of nearly 1.2 million people. Canada's largest city, Toronto, is also in Ontario, and it has a population of around 5.4 million. The second-largest city, Montreal, is in the province of Quebec, and it has a population of more than 3.7 million. Canada's third-largest city is Vancouver, on the west coast of the province of British Columbia, and it has a population of nearly 2.2 million.

How to say...

The Inuit people who live in the Nunavut province have their own language called Inuktitut.

How are you?	*Qanuipt*	(ka-nwee-peet)
What is your name?	*Kinauvit*	(kee-nau-veet)
thank you	*qujaanamiik*	(coo-yam-na-mee-ick)
yes	*Ii*	(ee)
no	*aakka or aagaa*	(ah-ka or Ah-ga)
goodbye	*tavvauvutit*	(tah-vow-vo-teet)

In a 2010 survey on quality of life in world cities, Vancouver was ranked fourth overall.

Economy

Canada has a strong **economy**. Traditional areas of employment include farming, fishing, logging, and manufacturing. The majority of manufactured goods are **exported**. In recent years, the government has invested in high-tech, modern industries. Modern technology also means that it is now very easy for people in **rural** areas to work from home.

Agriculture is also important in Canada. Wheat is the main crop, with nearly 4 percent of the world's wheat grown in Canada. Other crops include potatoes and apples. Incredibly, 60 percent of Canada's agricultural goods are exported to the United States.

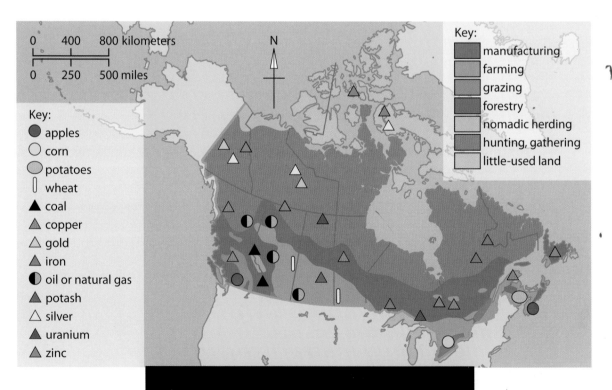

This map shows how the land in Canada is used for many different industries, including farming and mining.

Sustainability

In the Atlantic Ocean, off the coast of eastern Canada, stocks of cod fell dramatically in the 1990s because of overfishing. In some areas, fishing was banned completely to allow the stocks to recover. New fishing techniques, including **fish farms**, have also been introduced to help stabilize the fishing industry. The timber industry is another large employer in Canada. It is important that logging is also carried out in a **sustainable** way. New trees must be planted as often as old ones are cut down.

Natural resources

Canada's **natural resources** include oil, natural gas, and coal. Canada also has iron ore, nickel, lead, copper, and zinc deposits that are mined. Eighty percent of Canada's mined resources are exported. This includes uranium and diamonds. Uranium is used in the production of **nuclear energy**. More uranium is mined in Canada than anywhere else in the world.

Wildlife: Protecting Nature

Canada has 39 national parks. Banff National Park was the first of its kind in Canada. Located near the Rocky Mountains, the park is 2,564 square miles (6,641 square kilometers), and the stunning scenery includes snow-capped mountains, glaciers, forests, and Lake Louise. The park is also home to some of Canada's most famous wild animals, including **caribou**, wolves, and grizzly bears.

The smaller Forillon National Park is on the eastern tip of Quebec. It is a 94-square-mile (244-square-kilometer) landscape of steep cliffs, mountains, rivers, waterfalls, and forests. This protected area is rich in plant life, and 225 **species** of bird are found here, including jays, warblers, falcons, and owls.

There is amazing scenery in Banff National Park.

Polar bear capital of the world

The small town of Churchill, on the edge of Hudson Bay in Manitoba, is the place to see polar bears in Canada. People travel from all over the world to catch a glimpse of polar bears in their natural environment on the vast **tundra** nearby. When the ice freezes on the bay during the winter months, the polar bears spend all their time hunting seals. They need to eat as much as possible before the ice thaws and food becomes scarce.

Unfortunately, as climate change causes the temperature to increase, the time that the bears have to hunt on the ice is reduced. This is because the ice forms later in the year and melts sooner.

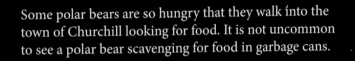

Some polar bears are so hungry that they walk into the town of Churchill looking for food. It is not uncommon to see a polar bear scavenging for food in garbage cans.

The power of water and wind

Canada is the second-largest user of **hydroelectric** power (HEP) in the world, after China. HEP uses moving water to create electricity, and hydroelectric power stations generate the most electricity in Canada. The country has been producing electricity in this way for more than 100 years. HEP is an excellent way to create power because it doesn't harm the environment in the way that burning **fossil fuels** does. Canada has many rivers and lakes where hydroelectric power can be produced.

Wind turbines can also be used to create clean, **renewable** energy. Much like the way that HEP uses water to create power, wind turbines use the natural power of the wind to generate electricity. There are now areas called wind farms that have collections of large wind turbines. Smaller wind turbines can be used on farms and even houses to supplement electricity from other, more traditional sources. Using wind power helps to reduce energy costs.

Environmental damage

Canada has large mining regions where there have been major problems concerning the environment. The water and soil have become polluted. Measures are now being taken to reduce this problem and to prevent further damage. In certain affected areas, trees have been planted to reduce the flow of polluted water over land. Along with natural plants that absorb polluting materials, these measures have resulted in fish returning to previously damaged rivers and lakes.

Recycling

As the population rises, landfill sites in Canada are becoming full, and new sites are needed to cope with the increase in waste. Recycling can help reduce the amount of waste entering landfill sites. Since the 1990s there has been a significant rise in the amount of recycling that is done, and households are now recycling more waste material than ever before.

This family is doing what it can to help the environment by recycling its household waste.

Infrastructure: Leaders, Health, and Schools

Canada's government is a **constitutional monarchy**. This means it has a king or queen as **head of state** (currently Britain's Queen Elizabeth II), but the monarch's power is limited by a **constitution**. Canada is also a **parliamentary democracy**. This means citizens elect representatives. These elected officials appoint high-ranking politicians such as the **prime minister**.

Senate and House of Parliament

A general election is held at least every five years to choose a new government. However, elections often take place more frequently. The Canadian government has a Senate and a House of **Parliament**. The Senate is made up of 105 members who represent their area or region. The House of Parliament has 308 members.

On a recent trip to Canada, Queen Elizabeth greets the crowds who have come to see her.

Member of the G8

Canada is a member of the **G8**, or Group of Eight. This group of wealthy countries, including the United States and the United Kingdom, meet once a year to discuss matters that affect global **economies**. The G8 representatives also discuss subjects ranging from climate change to diseases such as HIV/AIDS. Canada hosted the 2010 G8 summit in Huntsville, Ontario.

Health care

When people in Canada need to visit the doctor or go to the hospital, they do not have to pay. This is because they pay for their health care indirectly through taxes. In large cities such as Toronto, Montreal, and Vancouver, there are modern facilities and hospitals. The standard of health care is very high.

Daily life

Because of the huge size of the country, getting to a doctor can be difficult in remote areas. People have to travel many hours to receive medical treatment. In emergency cases, helicopters are used to get people to the nearest hospital.

In this remote, mountainous region in the province of Alberta, a rescue helicopter is used to help people in emergencies.

School life

Each province and territory of Canada has control over its own school system. In most regions, students attend school for 12 years. In Quebec they attend for 11 years. Education is **compulsory** until the age of 15 or 16 in most areas.

A typical elementary school day in the province of Nova Scotia starts at 8:05 a.m. and finishes at 2:05 p.m. Some of the children have breakfast at school. They have a 15-minute recess at 10 a.m., and lunch is at 12 p.m., for 30 minutes. Children have the option of taking a packed lunch or eating a school lunch.

These children are learning about zoology in school.

YOUNG PEOPLE

Because Canada is officially **bilingual**, most students at school learn a second language. French "immersion" classes are quite popular across the country. At these schools, all classes are conducted in French.

Higher education

There are 95 universities in Canada, as well as around 150 community colleges. Degrees take between 12 weeks and 4 years. Some people specialize in a certain area, such as forestry, art and design, or native studies.

Quebec has a **unique** education system. After secondary school, students spend two years studying at the Collège d'enseignement général et professionnel (CEGEP) before going on to college. Courses include social sciences and fine arts. Alongside their main studies, students must also take classes in topics such as literature, history, and physical education.

How to say...

French	*le français*	(luh fronsay)
English	*l'anglais*	(longlay)
art	*l'art*	(lar)
history	*l'histoire*	(listwah)
geography	*la géo(graphie)*	(la jayo(graffie))
math	*les mathématiques*	(lay mat-eh-mateek)
music	*la musique*	(la moozeek)

There are a wide variety of courses available at Canadian universities.

Culture: Singers, Stories, and Shrek

Justin Bieber performs in concert. He has fans all over the world.

The Inuit are internationally recognized for their traditional singing and dancing. Storytelling has also always been a big part of their culture. Stories have developed over thousands of years and often involve spirits of the sea and land. The Inuit are very proud of their art. Many images are created using bright colors to depict different aspects of Inuit life and the environment.

Music

Canadians listen to many different styles of music, including rock, pop, jazz, and folk. World-famous Canadian music stars include Leonard Cohen, Joni Mitchell, and Neil Young. The Canadian singer Justin Bieber became a worldwide star after appearing on YouTube in 2008.

In recent years, several female Canadian singers have had international success. Shania Twain has sold millions of albums with her mix of country and pop music. Alanis Morissette and Avril Lavigne have had international number-one albums. Perhaps the most famous Canadian female singer is Céline Dion. Her song "My Heart Will Go On" was featured in the 1997 movie *Titanic*.

GLENN GOULD (1932–1982)

Glenn Gould was a very popular and talented pianist. When he was only 15 years old, he performed in concerts, and he recorded his first album in 1955. He gave up performing in 1964 to concentrate more on broadcasting and recording.

Art: The Group of Seven

In 1920 seven artists decided that their art should have a **unique** Canadian style. They wanted to show Canada's beautiful **terrain** and rugged character. The group exhibited their art throughout the 1920s. The Group of Seven style is still very influential in **contemporary** Canadian art.

Lauren Harris painted this image of lakes and mountains in 1928.

Film

There are many famous Canadian actors, including Jim Carrey, Keanu Reeves, and Kiefer Sutherland. Many movies are made in Canada because costs are cheaper than in the United States. Toronto is often used instead of New York City, as the two cities are similar in size and have similar climates.

MIKE MYERS

(BORN 1963)

The comedian and actor Mike Myers was born in Scarborough, Ontario. He has appeared in the *Wayne's World* and *Austin Powers* movies and is famous as the voice of the animated ogre Shrek.

Literature

Canadian literature is well-known around the world. Lucy Maude Montgomery wrote *Anne of Green Gables* in 1908. This story of a young **orphan** girl is set in the area of Prince Edward Island, which then became very popular with tourists.

The novelist Margaret Atwood has a loyal following of readers all over the world. She won the Man Booker Prize in 2000 for her novel *The Blind Assassin*. The Sri Lankan–born Canadian writer Michael Ondaatje has also won this prize for his novel *The English Patient*, which became a hit movie in 1996.

Sports

During the winter, Canadians like to ski, snowboard, and ice skate. Ice hockey is the most popular sport in Canada. Every town has an ice rink, and major cities all have professional teams. These teams play in the United States National Hockey League (NHL). In 2010 Vancouver hosted the Winter Olympics.

During the rest of the year, many Canadians hike, canoe, and cycle around the country's rivers and lakes. Other sports that people enjoy are soccer, football, and baseball. **Lacrosse** is the official summer national sport of Canada, while ice hockey is recognized as the winter national sport.

Wayne Gretzky is the most successful ice hockey player in history.

Television and the Internet

Canadians have access to hundreds of channels on cable and satellite television. There are channels in English and in French. In 2009, 75 percent of the Canadian population had access to the Internet.

Food

Canadians have busy lives, and not everyone has time to cook a family meal every evening. Packaged meals, fast food, and restaurants are very popular. The types of food available in Canada are varied and have changed over time. In modern Canada, you can buy food from all over the world.

Canadians celebrate Thanksgiving in October. This is an important time when families come together and celebrate. Families cook a traditional meal of turkey, stuffing, cranberry sauce, squash, and potatoes. For dessert, there is usually pumpkin pie.

Maple syrup

One of Canada's most popular and famous foods is maple syrup. The syrup comes from the sap of maple trees, which grow in Quebec and Ontario. Native Canadians in the 1600s were the first to collect the sap, heat it, and transform it into syrup.

These buckets are used to collect sap from the maple trees. The sap is eventually turned into maple syrup.

Nanaimo bars

Ask an adult to help you make some delicious Nanaimo bars.

Ingredients—cookie layer

- 7 tablespoons unsalted butter
- 1/4 cup sugar
- 5 tablespoons cocoa powder
- 1 egg (beaten)
- 3 cups crushed graham crackers
- 1 cup finely chopped almonds
- 2 1/2 cups coconut

What to do—cookies layer

1. Melt the butter in a bowl over a pan of hot water.
2. Add the sugar and the cocoa powder and stir well.
3. Add the egg and stir until the mixture thickens. Remove from the heat.
4. Stir in the crushed graham crackers, chopped almonds, and coconut.
5. Press firmly into an ungreased 8-inch (20-centimeter) square pan.

Ingredients—cream layer

- 7 tablespoons unsalted butter
- 2 1/2 tablespoons heavy cream
- 2 tablespoons cornstarch
- 1 teaspoon vanilla extract
- 4 cups powered sugar

What to do—cream layer

6. Cream the butter, cream, cornstarch, vanilla, and sugar together well.
7. Beat until light. Spread over the cookie layer.

Ingredients—chocolate layer

- 3 1/2 ounces dark chocolate
- 3 tablespoons unsalted butter

What to do—chocolate layer

8. Melt the chocolate and butter over low heat. Leave to cool.
9. Once cool, but still liquid, pour over the cream layer.
10. Chill in the refrigerator until the chocolate layer has set.

Canada Today

Canada is an ever-changing country, and its major cities are growing in size and population. The increase of **immigrants** from other countries has led to great **diversity** in cities. Tourism is, and will continue to be, important to Canada. People visit from all over the world to explore the cities and experience the wildlife and landscapes.

Canadians love their sports, in particular ice hockey. They were especially pleased to beat their closest rivals, the United States, in the 2010 Winter Olympics in Vancouver.

Daily life

In the cold, harsh winters, Canadians are able to continue with their normal lives. In Montreal, for example, there is an underground shopping center. This means the shoppers do not have to deal with the freezing conditions as they move between work, stores, and movie theaters.

An important nation

Canada is a politically strong country. It is a member of the **G8** and the United Nations and works closely with other countries to find solutions to global problems. Canada also has an important trade agreement with the United States and Mexico, called the North American Free Trade Agreement (NAFTA). This aims to ensure that goods pass freely across the three countries.

The future

Canadians are very proud of their country and are often passionate about the natural beauty of Canada. It is very important that a balance can be found when using the **natural resources**. The country's future development needs to happen in a **sustainable** way, making sure that the natural surroundings of the country's wildlife remain undamaged for future generations.

Visitors from all over the world come to Canada to see Niagara Falls, which are amazing waterfalls.

Fact File

Official name:	Canada
Official languages:	English and French
Capital city:	Ottawa
Bordering country:	United States
Population:	34,030,589 (July 2011 est.)
Largest cities and populations:	Toronto (pop. 5.377 million); Montreal (pop. 3.75 million); Vancouver (pop. 2.197 million); Ottawa (pop. 1.17 million)
Urban population:	81%
Birth rate:	10.28 per 1,000 people
Life expectancy (total):	81.38 years
Life expectancy (men):	78.8 years
Life expectancy (women):	84.1 years
Ethnic groups:	British origin 28%; French origin 23%; Mixed 26%; Other European origin 15%; Other (Asian, African, Arab) 6%; Amerindian 2%
Religion:	Roman Catholic 42.6%; Protestant 23.3%; None 16%; Other Christian 4.4%; Muslim 1.9%; Other 11.8%
Internet users:	26.96 million
Military service:	voluntary

Type of government:	**constitutional monarchy, parliamentary democracy**
National animal:	Canadian beaver
National tree:	maple
Climate:	**temperate** in the south, subarctic and arctic (very cold) in the north
Total area:	3,855,103 square miles (9,984,670 square kilometers)
Land area:	3,511,023 square miles (9,093,507 square kilometers)
Water area:	344,079 square miles (891,163 square kilometers)
Mountains:	Logan; St. Elias; Lucania
Major rivers:	Mackenzie; Yukon; St. Lawrence
Highest elevation:	Mount Logan 19,551 feet (5,959 meters)
Lowest elevation:	Atlantic coast 0 feet (0 meters)
Currency:	Canadian dollar (C$)
Resources:	iron ore; nickel; zinc; gold; silver; diamonds; fish; timber; coal; petroleum, natural gas
Major industries:	processed and unprocessed minerals; food products; wood and paper; fish; petroleum; natural gas; transportation equipment; chemicals
Main imports:	machinery and equipment; motor vehicles and parts; crude oil; chemicals; electricity
Main exports:	industrial machinery; aircraft; telecommunications equipment; plastics; fertilizers; timber; aluminum; uranium; wheat

Famous Canadians

Margaret Atwood (author); Donavon Bailey (athlete); Justin Bieber (singer); Joseph Armand Bombardier (inventor); Michael Bublé (singer/songwriter); Kim Campbell (politician); Jim Carrey (actor); Linda Evangelista (model); Wayne Gretzky (ice hockey player); Avril Lavigne (singer/songwriter); Cluny Macphearson (inventor); Mike Myers (actor); Anna Paquin (actress); Keanu Reeves (actor); Jacques Villeneuve (race car driver)

National holidays

January 1	New Year's Day
March/April	Good Friday and Easter Monday
May	Victoria Day
July 1	Canada Day
September	Labor Day
October	Thanksgiving Day
November 11	Remembrance Day
December 25	Christmas Day
December 26	Boxing Day

National anthem

"O Canada" was adopted as the national anthem on July 1, 1980. The music was composed by Calixa Lavallée, and the original French lyrics were written by Adolphe-Basile Routhier. The official English lyrics are based on a version written in 1908 by Robert Stanley Weir. They are as follows:

O Canada!
Our home and native land!
True patriot love in all thy sons command.
With glowing hearts we see thee rise,
The True North strong and free!
From far and wide, O Canada,
We stand on guard for thee.
God keep our land glorious and free!
O Canada, we stand on guard for thee.
O Canada, we stand on guard for thee.

Academy Award–winner Anna Paquin is one of Canada's most famous actors. She is well-known for playing the character Rogue in the X-Men movies.

Timeline

BCE means "before the common era." When this appears after a date, it refers to the number of years before the Christian religion began. BCE dates are always counted backward.

CE means "common era." When this appears after a date, it refers to the time after the Christian religion began.

28,000 BCE	The first residents of what is now Canada arrive over the Bering Strait.
1000 CE	Vikings arrive from Scandinavia.
1497	Italian **navigator** John Cabot reaches the coast of Newfoundland.
1534	Jacques Cartier explores the St. Lawrence River and claims the shores of the Gulf of St. Lawrence for France.
1535	French **settlers** arrive to set up a **colony**, but many die during the winter and the attempt is abandoned.
1583	Newfoundland becomes England's first overseas colony.
1600s	A fur trade rivalry begins between the French, English, and Dutch. The Europeans form alliances with some of the native people.
1608	Samuel de Champlain establishes a colony in Quebec and founds "New France."
1670	Hudson's Bay Company is established by British traders.
1701	Forty First Nations chiefs sign a peace **treaty** with the French and the English, ending 100 years of war.
1756	The Seven Years' War begins between New France and the larger and wealthier British colonies. After early French successes, the settlement of Quebec falls in 1759, and the British advance on Montreal.
1763	Britain is given almost complete control of Canada.
1774	The Quebec Act recognizes the French language and the Roman Catholic religion in the colony. France is allowed to run Quebec.

1791	Quebec is divided into Lower Canada (present-day Quebec) and Upper Canada (present-day Ontario) to form the province of Canada.
1818	The 49th parallel becomes accepted as the border between the United States and Canada.
1857	Ottawa becomes the capital of the province of Canada.
1867	The provinces, including Ontario, Quebec, Nova Scotia, and New Brunswick, unite to become Canada. John A. Macdonald becomes the first **prime minister**. Over the next six years, the provinces of Manitoba, British Columbia, and Prince Edward Island are also included.
1885	The Canadian-Pacific railroad is completed
1896–1898	The Klondike Gold Rush begins along the upper Yukon River.
1914	World War I begins. Canada fights on the same side as Britain, France, and the United States.
1939	World War II begins. Canada fights again on the same side as Britain, France, and the United States.
1949	Newfoundland joins Canada.
1965	The present Canadian flag is adopted.
1971	The **Multicultural** Policy is declared.
1980	"O Canada" is proclaimed as Canada's national anthem, 100 years after it was first sung on June 24, 1880.
1982	The Canada Act and **Constitution** Act are signed, giving Canada control over future constitutional changes.
1991	Canadian forces participate in the Gulf War, following Iraq's invasion of Kuwait.
1992	The leaders of Canada, the United States, and Mexico agree to the terms of the North American Free Trade Agreement.
1993	Kim Campbell becomes the first female prime minister.
1995	A vote in Quebec rejects independence by a margin of only 1 percent.
1999	The territory of Nunavut is formed in northern Canada.
2010	Canada hosts the Winter Olympics in Vancouver and the **G8** summit in Huntsville, Ontario.

Glossary

Allies group of countries that fought together during World War II, including the United Kingdom, France, the United States, and Canada

autonomous mainly self-governed

bilingual able to speak two languages

caribou large deer

colony country ruled by another country

commodity something of use or value

compulsory when there is a requirement to do something

confederation union of areas to become one

constitution system of principles by which a country is governed

constitutional monarchy system of government in which a monarch (king or queen) is the head of state, but his or her power is restricted by a constitution

contemporary something that is of the present time

diversity having many different kinds or forms

economy all the produce and trade of a country

export sell goods to another country

fish farm business in which fish are bred and reared in captivity for selling as food

fossil fuel substance such as coal or oil that is burned for fuel

G8 group of wealthy nations, including Canada, the United States, and the United Kingdom, that meet every year to discuss issues affecting global economies, as well as issues such as disease and climate change

head of state person who is the chief representative of a country

hydroelectric electricity produced by water power

immigrant person who comes to live permanently in a foreign country

indigenous originating in a particular place

infrastructure basic framework of a country, such as government and schools

lacrosse game in which two 10-member teams try to hit a small ball into each other's netted goal. Each player has a stick with a netted pocket for catching, carrying, or throwing the ball.

multicultural representing many different cultures

natural resource naturally occuring material that people can use

navigator person who explores by sea

nuclear energy energy released from the center of tiny units called atoms

orphan child whose parents have both died

parliament ruling body of some countries; laws are made there

parliamentary democracy system of government in which citizens elect representatives, and these representatives, in turn, appoint high-level politicians such as the prime minister

prime minister head of a parliamentary government

prospector person who searches or explores for something valuable, such as gold

renewable able to be used over and over again without any loss of resources

rural having to do with the countryside

settler someone who moves to a country and establishes himself or herself there

species type of animal, bird, or fish

sustainable using a resource in a way that means it is not permanently damaged or depleted

temperate neither very hot nor very cold

terrain area of land that has natural features

treaty formal agreement between two states

tribe group of people who are linked by common ancestry

tundra huge area of treeless plain in the Arctic

unique only one of its kind

Find Out More

Books

Fiction

Montgomery, L. M. *Anne of Green Gables*. West Berlin, N.J.: Townsend, 2009 (first published in 1908).

Smucker, Barbara. *Underground to Canada*. Toronto: Puffin, 2008.

Nonfiction

Barlas, Robert, and Norm Tompsett. *Canada* (*Festivals of the World*). New York: Marshall Cavendish Benchmark, 2011.

Kalman, Bobbie. *Canada: The Culture* (*Land, Peoples, and Cultures*). New York: Crabtree, 2010.

Moore, Christopher. *The Big Book of Canada: Exploring the Provinces and Territories*. Plattsburgh, N.Y.: Tundra, 2003.

Williams, Brian. *Canada* (*Countries of the World*). Washington, D.C.: National Geographic, 2007.

DVDs

Anne of Green Gables (Sullivan Entertainment, 2002)

Websites

http://kids.nationalgeographic.com/kids/places/find/canada/
This website has games, videos, and articles all about Canada.

http://kids.yahoo.com
Type "Canada" into this search engine and find lots of photos, videos, and articles, as well as links to other great sites about Canada.

www.canadiangeographic.ca/kids/
You can find animal facts, games, maps, and more here!

Places to visit

If you are fortunate enough to visit Canada, here are some of the places that you could visit:

Niagara Falls, Ontario

A visit to the world-famous natural wonder of the Niagara Falls is a great way to start exploring the Great Lakes.

CN Tower, Toronto

One of the tallest towers in the world, CN Tower dominates the Toronto skyline. High-speed elevators take you to the top of the tower, where you can look out across the city in all directions.

Kluane National Park and Reserve of Canada

Visitors to this National Park can catch a glimpse of grizzly bears and black bears in their natural environment. The park is also home to Canada's tallest peak, Mount Logan.

Watch a live ice hockey match

You can watch a professional ice hockey match in every major city in Canada.

Topic Tools

You can use these topic tools for your school projects. Trace the map onto a sheet of paper, using the thick black outline to guide you.

The Canadian flag, with a big red maple leaf, was made the official flag of Canada in 1963. Copy the flag design and then color in your picture. Make sure that you use the right colors!

N

Ottawa

Index

Titles in the series